Confessions
From a
Call "Center" Girl

By
Donna Doherty

ISBN-9781679285820

INTRODUCTION

See if this sounds familiar. Let's say you have a burning question for a company that you have done business with for years. A place where you have been a loyal and satisfied customer. What do you do? Well, with the age of technology available at your fingertips, you can sign into your computer, smartphone, or tablet, then bring up the company's website. Once there, you review the entire menu and read all the FAQ's, but still do not find a definitive answer to <u>your</u> burning question.

Next, you go to "You Tube", do multiple searches hoping to watch any video that will give you a step-by-step answer that pertains to <u>your</u> question. Nothing!! Finally, you open discussions through texts and chats with family members, friends and co-workers, hoping that any one of them would be able to accurately answer <u>your</u> question, with full confidence and conviction. However, you get bits and pieces of responses that relate to <u>your</u> quintessential question, but nothing concrete. *UGH! Total frustration!*

So, *feeling defeated,* you're forced to take a *deep breath,* gather all your *courage and patience* that one can muster, and look up that 1-800 or local number of the company, and make that dreaded *CALL* to the Customer Service Center!

At first, you remain steady as you listen to the *long automated introduction* at the beginning of the call. When the *second automated phone prompt begins,* you feel your blood pressure start to rise, but you hold it together and hit the matching number needed to take you to the correct area. By the *third automated phone prompt,* you no longer want to answer or type your personal information, whether it be your account number, policy number, date of birth or phone pin. You just want to speak to a LIVE REPRESENTATIVE!!

But alas, you get that *awful final automated message* saying that your call has a wait time of 16 minutes and "will be answered in the order in which it was received". Really??? HHUUFF!!!

Even though you are now *completely aggravated* and on the *verge of a meltdown*, you must think fast! What do you do next? Do you wait the 16 minutes, hoping that others ahead of you will hang up, moving you up in the call que to a faster response? Or do you hang up and gamble on the hope of calling early the next day at the start of business hours for a much shorter response time?
What to do? What to do? HEELLLPPPP!!!!!

Well, you are in luck! This is the book that will finally divulge the *tips, tricks, secrets and confessions* to help move you faster through most of those annoying, automated phone prompts during your next phone call to many different companies.

<u>Some of the questions that you may be asking yourself (in order to *cut through the red tape*) when calling into a Call Center for Customer Service are:</u>

What are the "*magic words*" that will get me *directly* to a Call Representative, *without* having to type in everything on those endless phone prompts?

Why am I on hold forever waiting to talk to a human at one company, while getting through to a human immediately at another company?

Who are those voices on the other side of the line that are willing to answer my complex questions in a quick and concise manner?

Why is it that some Call Representatives give you a short, quick answer, then immediately ask "Is there anything else I can help you with today?" while others give you a long, drawn-out, conversational explanation at another company?

What is the best time to call a 24-hour Call Center... the morning, afternoon, evening, or during the overnight hours?

This book will provide very direct, definitive answers to those burning questions... and more!

It will also give you a juicy, revealing, and humorous behind-the-scenes look into the *secretive do's and don'ts* that must be followed by those friendly, faceless Customer Service Call Representatives on every answered call!!

Having been a Call Center Representative myself over a ten year period, in many different environments, I thought it would be fun to reveal some of my personal "**confessions**", giving you a clear bird's eye view, over the wall, and into those brick and mortar buildings that house the "Call Centers".

We'll take a look into the shenanigans that the Representatives and Supervisors continuously face during their shifts, as well as the hilarious stories we have all shared in dealing with the customers, the computers, the headsets, and the call ques!

So, relax, (maybe grab a glass of wine), settle in, and enjoy this informative, funny, quirky, behind-the-scenes look into

The Wonderful World of Customer Service… via the Call Center!

Thank you for calling …!
How may I help you today?

CHAPTER ONE – "WHO'S THAT CALL "CENTER" GIRL?"

In most cases, **"She"** is a real go-getter, and has done everything she can to keep moving forward in her life. She's a consistent doer, firmly digging in her heels to perform each task at hand with precision and grace. She's a determined worker, going from job to job to move herself forward in pay, while also accommodating the needs of her family at home. She's a dreamer, who mindfully maps out the wonderful transitions that will be in her future.

She's intuitive, quickly reading happiness or sadness on the faces of others. She's kind, and has a big heart, especially when empathizing with those who have struggled. She's smart, despite only having earned a limited high school or "some college" education.

She's usually a good girl, always trying to do the right thing while following the rules, obeying the authorities, and keeping herself in check. She's a planner, keeping the bills and budget intact, while also organizing special dinners or game nights with friends. She's a scheduler, constantly juggling the dates and days to suit everyone's hectic work and school commitments.

"She" is the one who currently "sits" attached to a desk with half walls in a professional setting (8 hours or more, except on breaks, when she can stand and/or walk). She wears a headset and a microphone, answering call after call from those needing her help immediately, regarding a product, a complaint, a widget, an experience, or any other information..., prompting very decisive answers. The calls drive her to accurately read from her script, as she strives to stay calm, talk in a low tone, provide a timely solution, all while checking off the list of key points for quality assurance, in the middle of a loud, stressful, Call Center environment!!

(It's no wonder, she often thinks,
"Oh Calgon...take me away!!")

After doing my homework for this book, I learned that **"She"**, the "U.S. Call Center Girl", is actually the average age of 49, divorced or never been married, is providing the main support for her children as a single mother, usually has had some previous medical issues, but must continue to work to be self-supportive, with less than $2,000 in savings.

However, this "Girl" is full of knowledge, experience, virtues, and... grit!

So, the question begs,
"IF SHE'S ALL THAT AND MORE, THEN WHAT EXACTLY HAPPENED TO TURN THIS TALENTED WOMAN INTO A **CALL CENTER GIRL????????**
(The answers may just surprise you!!)

<u>Now, for the Disclaimer:</u> Although there are plenty of Fabulous, Handsome, Knowledgeable and Kind <u>MEN</u> that work in the Call Centers, I have chosen to focus on the <u>WOMEN</u>. Why? Well, mainly because that is what I am, and in this book, I will be providing the perspective of my own personal experiences, as well as relatable stories from my female co-workers. However, I do smell a juicy, informative sequel! I'm currently continuing my extensive research and interviews to find out what it's like to be a CALL

CENTER BOY, from a male representative's point of view!! It should be interesting... so stay tuned!!

However, in the meantime, back to *this* book...

CHAPTER TWO – "THE FINANCIAL BACKGROUNDS"

So, who exactly is **"She"** in the context of this book? **"She"** is an amalgam of all the women (no matter what their age) who have ended up becoming "Call Center Girls" in a Call Center building (or in her own home working remote.) Hers is not a unique story. There are many factors that can lead such a talented, smart, friendly, knowledgeable, aging woman, to accept a work offer and find herself *seated* in a Call Center or Contact Center. Her journey through life, and the many choices that she has chosen along that journey, (or had to endure) have either "successfully made" or "horribly broken" her financial future.

Historically, I've discovered through my research that the most common factors that most US Women have continued to create a stable, financial future for themselves, *and keep it, are:*

- **Working as a single woman** until her late 60's, never marrying.
- **Obtaining a full college education** early in life, then working and saving money for 10-15 years before marrying, having children, and/or becoming an at home Mom.
- **Investing early** in a 401K plan, or another retirement plan, and keeping the funds intact until she retires.
- **Inheriting wealth** from parents, siblings, a dead spouse, or the proverbial "rich uncle" (or aunt).
- **Marrying a well-off spouse** who will support her sufficiently throughout her marriage, or pay out a substantial amount of alimony after the divorce.
- **Being that Lucky One** who ends up finding the buried treasure, winning the lottery, having the right numbers on the big race at the track, hitting the mega jackpot at a casino, becoming a member of the Kardashian clan (wait, what?), or investing heavily in a stock that

splits, doubling or tripling that initial amount. These last items are all long shots, but may become possibilities, at the right time and place.

With all of that said, just like *"good luck"* may help a woman achieve financial independence, there are even more *"catastrophic situations"* that can <u>ruin</u> a woman's financial future, even after she's planned well for that future. Here are just a few that I have personally seen affect the women in my life:

- **Medical Bills** – as women, it is the #1 reason why we file for bankruptcy, either from our own health problems, especially if older, or from our family members.
- **Loss of a Good Job** – as women, especially in the middle class, we have relied upon the many yearly increases in our corporate and retail establishments to keep up with our expenses. However, over the past 10 years, it is rare to hear of women that have been able to retain both their position, *and* their well-paying salary increases. Downsizing, furloughs, becoming underemployed at a lower salary, or working shorter shifts, has made it difficult to meet the bills. Many of these women are also single Moms who become desperate, taking any job they can get in Call Centers, Convenience Stores, Fast Food Restaurants, Cleaning Companies, etc., just to continue to have any income at all through honest work, and still provide for their families at home.
- **Loss of a Spouse** –for a woman, this can occur through divorce or death. The loss can be especially hard when the children are young. If there is a lack of child support payments or life insurance payments to continue the same lifestyle, the changes can be devastating to a woman and her family. No matter how hard she works, there may be no time to recover, especially if the loss has occurred later in her own life. Downsizing her home is usually the only option to go forward.
- **Spending Too Much** – as women, we like to "decorate", not only our homes, but our faces with make-up, our nails with polish, our hair with highlights and wigs, our bodies with nice clothes, jewelry

and tattoos, and our outside environments with plants, flowers, bushes and trees. All of this "decorating" costs money, lots of it, in addition to the regular monthly expenses that we <u>need</u> to pay.

- **Making Too Little** – as women, we also continue to make much less at most jobs compared to men in the same positions. Couple that fact with our "need" to pay the bills and our "wanting" to decorate. Our salaries are often not enough to accomplish both, even if we work the overtime hours, or get a 2nd job in the final shift when we eventually get home, taking care of the cooking, cleaning, laundry, our family, any random errands, as well as the personal maintenance on ourselves, to try and stay young, fresh and healthy. Whew! All this rushing around and mental stress worrying over money is often a drain on our physical and mental abilities, further diminishing our health over time.

- **Sharing, Donating, Helping** – as women, we are (usually) compassionate and social people. We like to be included in the lives of our family, friends and churchgoers. Sometimes that means we lend, or simply hand over our hard-earned money to those who are struggling more than ourselves. This makes us empathetic, kind, and frankly, human. However, when we continue to give away our small amount of savings for the sake of others, we eventually become the "needy people" ourselves later in life, especially when it is so much harder for us to continue to work outside of the home, and/or our health begins to fail.

- **Focus on the Present** – when we women don't start that Savings Account in our teens, or that 401k Retirement Plan in our twenties, or those CD deposits/Mutual Funds/Stocks or Bonds during our thirties, we tend to keep living in the moment with our money. So, as time rolls by, we may have lots of "things" that we have acquired, and lots of "experiences" that we will remember, but we don't have any MONEY to sustain our lifestyle and our health.

- **Vices** – finally, when we as women continually give in to our demons and impulses, we tend to eat out too much, or get drinks with friends too often, or vacation too lavishly, or gamble too much, or shop impulsively for unnecessary items. Such behaviors are often the symptoms of some deeper insecurities. If they are indulged on a regular basis, they can become quite the norm, completely ruining our lives, as we burn through our precious finances.

When any of these life changing, catastrophic occurrences (or bad habits) unwillingly become a part of our lives, they can be disastrous blows to our present and future financial well-being.

So, what if **"She"** does encounter any or all of those hardships or habits during her lifetime? What's a woman to do? Well, **"She"** can pick herself up, dust herself off, pull up her boot straps (or the straps on those cute sling-back stilettos), update that resume,' put on her best outfit, and go out and find where she can use her veritable wisdom, determination, worthiness and people skills to dive in and restart her career all over again... ***in a real hurry***...hence, the Call Center!

CHAPTER THREE - "THE GOOD THINGS"

So why take that job in a Call Center at all?

Well, the good news is that most Call Centers often have "job fairs" and "hire on-the-spot" for their Customer Service Representative positions. After passing a drug test, you can usually begin a week later, eliminating a lot of the 3-4 week wait times required to interview, test and be hired at other jobs.

Also, Call Centers also usually have paid training classes, often for 4-6 weeks, which means you will be earning money immediately, without the stress of meeting quality assurance or sales quotas during the training days. However, you may have to meet weekly assessment (test) grades (70% or greater) to maintain your employment during training.

Another plus, at the end of the day, you can leave the job at work, without finishing anything at home, or being on call through your cell phone or email. This eliminates being threaded to your job all day and night!

Being able to work a specific shift that fits your needs is also a big factor for those that are trying to meet the needs of their family, while also bringing in an income. Or maybe it is your second job, where you can earn extra money after putting in a full 8 hours elsewhere. Or maybe it is that graveyard shift that is so hard to find but fits your nocturnal lifestyle (and the differential percentage pay that goes along with it!). Whatever the reasons, being able to get the shift you want within a 24-hour cycle in a secure, air-conditioned building is something that can be invaluable to a Call Center employee.

As a Representative (Rep. for short), it may be easy for you to move up quickly in a Call Center if you follow all the rules on a daily basis. That's because there is often a lot of attrition (people often leaving or being let go) in Call Centers, usually based upon bad performance, poor attendance or just plain boredom and misconduct. So, if there is an opening for a Help Desk or Supervisory position, you can usually get an immediate interview if your performance is up to par and you are willing to put in the extra hours needed for coverage and meetings.

Friendships formed in a Call Center are unique. They're usually based upon the shift that you currently work or have worked in the past. I have often been the one to get the "Happy Hour Crowds" together after a swing shift or a graveyard shift.

After the swing shift (3pm-11pm), we usually ended up at a bar for the last two hours before last call. After the graveyard shift (11pm-7am), we usually ended up at a diner, eating breakfast and discussing the weirdest calls of the night. Either way, it's nice to be able to socialize and talk to one another occasionally, instead of just the customers. I pride myself on still socializing with, or remaining in contact with, many of my former co-workers from years past. Precious!

Next, the benefits at a Call Center are usually pretty good. As long as you are working a full time schedule, you may be eligible for medical, dental, vision and life insurance, as well as short/long term disability, a flexible spending program and a 401K retirement plan, depending upon the company and its standards.

Finally, the calls in a Call Center are usually categorized as "Scripted" or Non-Scripted". A "Scripted Call" involves reading an opening script verbatim when answering a call, then using other scripts to answer any other questions on the call. For instance, if a customer has called in to report a lost credit card, you would use the "opening script" when you answer the call, then use the "lost/stolen script" to obtain the answers needed for you to fill out the data on a computerized lost/stolen report.

Some Call Centers may provide this redundant "Scripted Format" only at an entry level position. This is because some workers, especially older workers, find this format to be the best, with a feeling of contentment in their position. They usually remain employed longer, since they are not being pressured into learning new software programs for other call type segments. Many have no interest in moving ahead in the company. As a result, their salaries remain at a lower level, with only minimal yearly increases.

A "Non-scripted Call" involves reading only the opening script verbatim, then answering the remaining questions *in your own words*. For instance, if a customer wants quotes on group van rides vs. private car rides to the airport, you could look up each type of ride and answer the customer using your own knowledge and appropriate terminology, without using any scripts. This is helpful to the employees who want the freedom to provide their best customer service using their own experiences and judgement, without having to refer to pre-written words for every answer. They are also the candidates that are given more training in additional call segments, earn higher bonuses, and are given higher evaluation scores, and higher yearly raises, when they excel at their practices.

So as you can see, if you are a dedicated worker looking for any of the above criteria in your next position, and you're willing to follow all the rules and regulations set forth by the company, then a Call Center position may be just the right fit for you! Go for it!

CHAPTER FOUR – "THE ABC'S OF IT ALL"

During my research for this book, I found some eye-opening facts relating to the current trends at the Call Centers.

For instance, at *some* companies, like Zappos and Microsoft, there are several ways that the Call Center Reps. can be taking orders or giving out information within a relaxed, playful environment. They can wear different costumes, take breaks to bicycle around outside, shoot hoops on the courts on campus, or get free food and drinks from the cafeteria. These perks provide the workers with some Zen time and a healthy corporate environment.

However, at some Call Centers, the limiting, and sometimes demeaning rules and regulations that are used, are very similar to what I had to *unwillingly* follow during my nine years at Catholic School (before I switched to Public School). Now, I'm sure these restrictions are similar at the Protestant schools, the Hebrew schools, the Muslim schools, the Day schools, and any other educationally formatted place, where the teachers can be a little stricter than other schools. The rules can be domineering, and the consequences can be quite cruel, if the rules are not obeyed... religiously!

Here are a few examples of the rules that I have personally adhered to similarly in *my* two environments: **Catholic School vs. the Call Center**:

At **Catholic School**, you must obey the start time rules by arriving early, setting up your books on your desk, and getting ready to be properly seated, after putting away your coat in the "cloak room", (and pants too if you were a girl and it was cold or snowing outside, and you were not allowed to wear your pants underneath your uniform skirt within the school walls!) Really?...WTF!

At the **Call Center**, you must arrive early, check the daily break time listing posted on the board or online, clock in within seven minutes of your start time, bring up all of your programs, put on your headset and be properly seated and ready for your first call. If these rules are not followed explicitly on a daily basis, you may be in for big trouble, and possibly be written up.

{Disclaimer: Recently, many of the Call Centers have been taken to task on this start time issue. The employees began suing for overtime, claiming that they were being forced to have their programs up and be fully ready to take their first call BEFORE CLOCKING IN on their start time. This is called "working off the clock" and is illegal in most states, if it goes beyond the standards of the National Labor Law for hourly workers. This Law states in part that there is no overtime paid for starting 7 minutes before your shift time, as well as not being considered late, 7 minutes after your shift time. Many Reps. are in multiple call segments and are also in a "hotel environment" (no standard desk assigned as their own.) They need 10 or 15 minutes to find a working desk/chair/computer, and then bring up all their programs to be ready for that first call in any segment. Asking to have this all done prior to the start of the shift, and then clocking in, is an issue that the Reps. have prompted legal action on to protect their rights, and their jobs.

Similar suits have been brought against companies by employees of any environment that require them to answer their emails and cell phones, before or after their working hours. The lawyers have been diligent about bringing this issue to the attention of the public so the employees can be aware of their rights regarding this practice.}

So how will all these trending issues be resolved? Stay tuned! Now, back to the list!

At **Catholic School**, you must arrive *early or on time* and not be *late* for the start of school. If you do arrive late, it usually sparks a trip to the Principal's office for a stern warning or worse.

At the **Call Center**, you can be penalized *more* for coming in *late*, (8 minutes after the shift time), than for being absent for the entire day (as long as you have PTO (Paid Time Off) hours available to utilize). This penalty for being late is usually posted into your quarterly evaluation, which can lower your bonus amount. It also opposes the normal procedure of most companies, which appreciate you coming into work at all, and allow you to make up the time when late at the end of your shift.

At **Catholic School**, you must listen to, not only your own teacher, but the other teachers or principals, who may be monitoring your classroom during the day.

At the **Call Center**, you must listen to substitute supervisors from other shifts, who are often cold and standoffish. They can become your "boss for the day", leaving much opportunity for them to reign power and dictate authority over the normally accepted behaviors of the Reps. on their regular shift.

At **Catholic School**, we're taught to face front, be attentive, remain seated, and NOT to talk to your "neighbors" in the classroom.

At the **Call Center**, the same… otherwise you could be in big trouble.

At **Catholic School**, you must wear the standard uniform, with no variations (i.e. hem of the skirt must be below the knee and may be measured with a ruler by the nuns); the bow tie must be straight and clasped; the bolero (vest), (with the school emblem sewn in straight and pressed), must be large enough to cover your female budding breasts. (Talk about body shaming...Yikes!).

At the **Call Center**, there are usually pictures of the type of clothes that are OK to wear, vs. not OK. The biggest issue that I've personally seen at every one of them has been the women's shoes. The closed vs. open-toed shoe, the height of the heel, and a slippery sole vs. a rubber sole (for safety reasons). Also, the strapping ties going up the leg, as well as the colors and patterns on the shoes, may be perceived as risqué or promiscuous. It can drive a person mad!

There's also the "temperature determinant". What is that you say? Well, since it's so hot during the spring and summer months in FL, AZ, NV and other states, the high temperature of the day can determine whether long, thigh-length shorts may be worn instead of pants or a skirt (despite being in an air conditioned building). In theory, this sounds like a fair policy delegated to a trivial, petty issue. However, since most Call Centers revolve around a 24-hour period, your shift time can determine which high temperature would personally affect you regarding your choice of wearing shorts or not. You would not believe how this issue can cause such adversity among the employees, especially when you have day vs. night shift workers justifying whether they are correct in making their assessment on what to wear that day. Forget world hunger, foreign wars and the number of homeless people out there, this is a REAL HARROWING PROBLEM!!

Along with all of the previous fashion issues listed above, if you also include the incorrect height and/or fabric of a capri pant (mid-calf), or the low, plunging V-neck on any assorted blouse or sweater, these fashion faux pauxs could easily get you sent home without pay for the day. Any blatant behavior that continues in this manner, can cause you big trouble, including being written up or fired.

At **Catholic School**, you must watch what you say, the way you say it, and not curse at all. If you disobey by shouting, screaming, crying or acting out, you could be sent to the Mother Superior's office for a "paddling." ("Paddling" is a form of corporal punishment that was allowed back in the day, where a big, flat wooden paddle was brought out, and the student had to bend over while the nun hit you several times on the behind with the paddle; it was legal for the school to provide this service if your parents signed the waiver not to sue the school; well, my parents *gladly* signed that paper every year, thinking this punishment was necessary to keep my sister and I in line. Seriously? Thanks Mom and Dad for those legal "sore days"!!).

At the **Call Center**, your communication on the phone, or with the management team, is the primary function of your job. Your words, your tone, your breaths and your calmness during a stressful call, are all indicators of whether or not you are adequate enough to perform this job on a daily basis. And if you curse at all, at a customer or a member of management, you could get in big trouble, or fired immediately...Bye-Bye!

So, as you can see, what I learned early in life at a Catholic School, can easily be applied to several of the bigger rules later in life, especially at a Call Center.

If you were one of the good kids in school that followed most of the rules and stayed in your lane, you most likely would do well in a Call Center environment (and I did!).

However, if you were one of the f...-ups, the ones that continually messed with the teacher, so she had to walk over and yell at you, pretty much on a daily basis; or if you were constantly sent to the Principal's office for some "discipline", and things haven't changed much; then the Call Center is definitely _not_ the place for you! Nuff said!

CHAPTER FIVE – "MAKING THAT CALL"

There are many more "**secrets**" that are hidden inside of a Call Center.

First, there are the "**secrets**" geared toward YOU, the customer, aimed at giving you the savvy ways to master the tips and tricks to (hopefully!) have a quick and easy experience when calling into a Call Center.

After you have tried the Websites, Webchats and Apps for the company, but to no avail, and you still cannot get a definitive answer to your burning question, it's time to bite the bullet and make the CALL to the Call Center. However, before doing so, here's a few "**secrets**" to use *before* dialing that number or after:

- Gather all the information that the Rep. will need from you to verify who you are and what you are asking for. Depending upon the company your calling, please have your account number, policy number, last four of your social security number, date of birth, current address, email address, credit, debit or checking account number, as well as the expiration date and CVV number ON the card (if needed), and the important question ready to go that you need answered. This will *save you both scads of time* in receiving the most proficient answer in a quick manner.

- Go to some of the best websites or apps that can help you "hack" the *phone prompts*, letting you *bypass* them to get to a human quickly. For instance, (at the time of this writing), you can use the Gethuman app for Android and iOS phones which is still *free* to access "phone bypasses" for many businesses. However, the Gethuman.com website now *charges* for access.)

- <u>Dialahuman.com</u> for *free* access to several popular businesses and their listed "phone bypasses". They will allow you to go past the phone menus and directly to a human at the Call Center. Another site is <u>WhatIs.com/Bypass Ivrs, Talk to a Real Person</u> which is similar in their "phone bypasses" for certain companies.
- Do your research! Some Customer Service numbers beginning with 1-800, 1-855, 1-866, etc. are starting to *charge*, if dialed from a mobile phone. In that case, try to use a landline phone or webchat online to keep the contact *free.*
- Once the number is dialed, try the old standby method of pressing the number 0 for the operator. Or you can try 0* or *0 on a landline phone, or 0# or #0 on a mobile phone.
- Try just staying *silent*, "pretending" you have a rotary phone and it may bypass directly to a Rep. But beware, some companies have become wise to this trick. The call may hang up if no one is heard on the line.
- As soon as the auto phone prompt begins, say "Representative" several times into the phone over the prompt, or additional prompts. It may end the questions and put you through to the Rep.
- Choose the "Spanish" option at the beginning of the call for a shorter wait time. Most of those Reps. are Bi-lingual and can help you in English if you tell them you mistakenly pushed the wrong option for a Rep.

Good Luck and remember...lots of deep breaths and plenty of patience will be the key to maintaining your composure during the call!

CHAPTER SIX – "WHO'S CALLING PLEASE?"

So far, this book has focused on the calls that the customer has initiated themselves, looking to call INTO the Call Center, and wanting assistance from a Customer Service Rep. regarding their questions on a product or service.

However, what should one do when the call comes TO the customer FROM a telemarketer? Which answer would you choose?

A – Listen to the pitch and not be rude in interrupting the speaker

B – Say "I'm not interested" and hang up

C – Say "Please do not call again" and hang up

Well, the correct answer depends upon your previous or current relationship with the company calling you. For a better understanding, let's dive deeper into these responses.

A – The **"secret"** is that this answer may be correct, say if you have purchased a car with a dealership, either recently, or in the past. They may be calling back to verify your satisfaction with the car, or to have you upgrade to a newer model. However, if it's a company you've never heard of, or have no interest in, see the answer for C below. If you *are* interested in the details of this new company and product, have the Rep. *give you* a call back number for you to call, or a physical address, or an email address for the company, and do your own research. DO NOT give out any of your personal information to an unfamiliar caller. If they have *none* of the company information that you've requested from them, it's probably a SCAM, and hang up.

B – This answer may be considered firm, fair and direct to the telemarketer. However, most Reps. working for legitimate companies must "categorize" their calls, especially the short ones. (This legitimizes the conversation on a recorded call.) When, you the customer, just say, "I'm not interested", the **"secret"** is that most companies will still allow another 4-5 calls back to you the customer under that "Not Interested" category response. To stop the calls entirely, use answer C below.

C – This **"secret"** answer is the one to use when you want to *stop the calls entirely on that particular sale or promotion*. The company Rep. usually must categorize the call in a "Do not Contact" category. But remember, even if you *are* on a "National Do Not Call List", companies that have a relationship with you through prior purchases or usage, may still be able to contact you, depending upon your "Privacy" settings with those companies and their affiliates. If you are not sure what those Privacy settings are, give each company a call. The **"secret"** here is that most legitimate companies will let you "Opt out" of being contacted on certain sales and promotions, if it's allowed in your Privacy setting. They will usually send you something to sign and send back regarding the Privacy policy. This will be the legal proof acknowledging your wishes.

It's funny, with all of the technology available on our computers, tablets and smartphones that can track us wherever we are or wherever we are going, I'm still amazed by the amount of "scoundrels" who are out there "hiding behind desks", wanting to weasel their way into our lives through *devious* phone calls.

Many companies rely on "robots" to do their dirty dialing on complex computer programs. The **"secret"** is that the "robots" can even provide local area codes on your Caller ID, even though they may be located far from your actual area. They continue to call down a list of phone numbers until someone answers the phone. Then, the Rep. retrieves the call and chimes in as a live person, pushing the latest product to sell, or pulling a horrendous SCAM. Quick and efficient for the companies, but annoying as hell for the customers, who must answer or screen those "mystery" calls *all day long*!

So, as in any business transaction, *let the buyer beware*!!
Remember, stay smart and savvy! Do your own research before handing over any personal information or credit card numbers!

CHAPTER SEVEN – "WHAT IS MY SALARY?"

As I continued with my research for this book, I learned about the income and hiring trends that have been used by many of the US customer service industries over the past several years. For instance, the majority of Inbound Customer Service Representatives and Tele Service Agents are female... while the higher paying Tech Support, Help Desk and Sales Support positions in the industry are held by males.

From the U.S. Department of Labor, Bureau of Labor Statistics dated May 2014, regarding the numbers for some US Call Centers, the report stated in part:

Arizona, in particular the Phoenix-Mesa area, had the highest occupations ratio, with a location quotient of 9. This means more people were employed in the Customer Service Representative industry in that area than any other. It's also considered to be the "Call Center Heaven" in that state, as well as part of the "Pink Collar Ghetto," (lower income female dominated positions).

In the same study, Florida was ranked the 2nd highest state that employed Customer Service Representatives. The Tampa Bay/St. Petersburg area was 9th out of 10th for employment of a Customer Service Representative, per metro area. Despite the higher level of employment of CSR's in that state, it had the lowest hourly wage at an avg. $15.24, out of the top avg. hourly wage of $19.90 an hour in New York for the same position.

Interesting, considering my personal wage as a Customer Service Representative in Florida was worse. I had a starting wage that was much, much lower than those stated, during the same time frame (2014).

Today, some companies still only have a starting salary at the bare minimum wage (currently $7.25 or $8.25 an hour in several states). However, most companies only pay slightly above that amount ($9.00 - $11.00 an hour). Hardly enough to live on in today's society. Also, since many "excellent employees" can spend 20-30 years in a Call Center, the reported average wage is often skewed by those long term employees' hourly wages and bonuses, which can average at a much higher rate per hour (sometimes double the actual starting wage of a new employee).

The good news is that the opportunities to join a Call Center are quite abundant in certain parts of the country. And it is easier to be hired quickly and begin earning money in those positions than most other jobs!

So, let's say you impressed everyone in the interview, passed the assessment, and the drug test. Congratulations, you're hired as a Rep.! Great! But are you full time, part time, working days or nights? This is where it gets sticky!

There's a "**secret**" that has recently trickled down to the workforce. It's this: Several companies are now using different terms for **"New Hire Employment"** and **"Job Type"** on their applications. These terms often describe the classification of the job, which determines your hours, your wages and your benefits (or lack of them). I slowly became aware of this trend after going through several job searches and interviews myself at various service industries.

Besides the original US standard of *Full-Time* status, usually 40 hours per week, which normally includes benefits, here are some of the **"tweaked Job Types"** that are currently being advertised to new hires, mostly *without* benefits:

Part-Time, may be up to 35 hours per week, but mostly only 20-28 hours per week, since many industries now consider anything over 28 hours to be Full Time, which constitutes possibly paying out benefits.

Contract, which is specialized employment for only a few weeks or months; it could be any number of hours a week at a higher rate of pay, but only for a *limited time.*

On Call, usually *limited hours* on a part time shift, but you must be available whenever the company "calls" you in, at any time, on any given day, in order to make any money.

Extra Board, similar to On Call, but this job is usually only for the *limited big events* such as weddings, conventions, banquets, holiday parties, etc.; you are only needed during peak busy times that require "all hands on deck"; depending upon the industry and your location, you could be working every night, or you could go weeks without being called in at all.

Temporary, usually *filling in* for a permanent employee for a limited time (maternity leave, military leave, a sabbatical, etc.); you know from the start that you will only be there for a week, a month, or a bit longer.

Seasonal, which is a *limited time*, usually only 4-8 weeks in any industry, during peak seasons only; think working at a store through the Christmas season, or at a pool over the summer, or at a ski lodge during the winter.

When applying for any of these **"Job Types"**, most people are completely unaware of the *meanings* of these "hourly terms" until they are actually at the HR office signing papers. This is when their heads start spinning, as they try to quickly calculate how much money they would actually be taking home in their weekly, bi-weekly, monthly, or random occasional paycheck, before they begrudgingly accept the position and sign their name on the dotted line, just to be employed.

Compounding the **"Job Type"** problem is the **"Upsell Tactic"**. Currently, in positions such as bank tellers, pest control reps., credit card reps., cable company reps., and alike, there are **"Upsell Quotas"** that must be met to maintain your level, or even keep your position, within the company. This seemingly friendly way of suggesting an increase in the price paid, pitching additional products or the number of products to the customer in a nonchalant manner, and actually closing the deal, has become the norm for the CSR"s who want to keep their level, or pay and/or job in these industries!!!

Now, for the brighter side! If one, or two, or thousands of the leaders over these worker bees decided to change the way their hours and profits are allocated, mainly among *all* of the employees, it would give way to distributing the raises, stock options, profit-sharing and promotions, more evenly. In turn, this would promote loyalty to the company again, which would *finally* start trending a better financial picture for the worker bee again. Yay!

The best example of this is the CEO of a US company that raised all the salaries to $70,000, for those doing the same job. This was an increase from an avg. $35,000 a year! Fingers crossed... this scenario continues to multiply very, very soon!

CHAPTER EIGHT – "BY THE NUMBERS"

Next, are the "**behind-the-scenes secrets**" that affect **the Rep.** on each recorded call, while she casually has a pleasant conversation with you, manages her computer screens, and keeps her eye on the time, to all meet the mathematical equation that's allotted to her per call. Yikes!

The most important job factors that affect the "Call Center Girl" on a minute to minute basis are: Quality Assurance (grading the calls on behavioral do's and don'ts), AHT (actual handle time or length of the call) and ADH (adhering to her personally scheduled breaks posted by management for the day).

Most outsiders are unaware of the strict standards that are applied to an employee on a minute to minute basis in a Call Center. There are daily metrics used in determining the representative's progress and monetary value within the company, and they can be mind boggling!! Here's a brief break down:

First, there are the **"personal metrics"** that must be adhered to by the Rep. (representative) each day in order to meet the criteria set by the Call Center. Things such as the Rep's start time, break times, lunch time, meeting times, coaching times, bathroom times (*yes, I said it*), ending time and *required overtime*, all must be met daily, and quite proficiently. Most of these "times" are assigned <u>3-digit codes that must be input into the phone or computer</u> by the Rep. at the end of one call, but right before the next call comes in (usually within 5 seconds, sometimes 3 seconds) in order to "Finish that call" or actually "Take that break"! Any diversion, either by a couple of seconds, or a couple of minutes, on any given day or days, can make or break a rep's "ADH"..., and further employment within the company.

Next, there are the **"call metrics"**, used in examining the "Quality Assurance" and "AHT" on every call. Factors such as these can add stress to the rep., as she quickly and accurately adheres to the following while on the call:

- Using the proper tone of voice at the greeting; (high and cheerful)
- Executing the best listening and answering skills required
- Keeping track of the details of the conversation that must be vocally answered and manually input into the computer, while never expressing a deep breath or sigh while doing so
- Using the correct resources to convey the accurate answers to the customer during the call (Guides, Notes, Standard Operations)
- Remaining calm while speaking on an escalated call
- Meeting the requirements of reading the pre-written scripts at the beginning and at the end of the call, including the sign off statement
- "Following the rules" in regard to the product, information or complaint (you can say this, but you can't say that) to avoid any "deductions" on the call
- Totaling the competency portions on the checklist for the entire call (which usually must produce a score of 90-100% accuracy per call)
- Answering the standard number of calls per day (can be from 85 to 120 calls on a full-time shift) and meet the required status of "AHT"

- Meeting the overall scores needed on the 8-10 monthly monitored calls, picked by the folks in "Quality Assurance" to reach the quarterly bonus

A "slip up" on any of these factors can sabotage the rep.'s performance, monetary perks (bonuses) and entire employment time spent at the facility. Talk about pressure!

On one call, one large error, or several small errors, regarding any one of the previously listed factors, can make or break a rep's employment, especially during her first 90 days on her "probationary period". Add to that the pressure of having to sell or upsell a product to meet a daily or weekly quota, as well as having knowledge of a staggering amount of "do's and don'ts" that must be learned and applied quickly and efficiently on every call. All these rules can have a profound effect on the "quality grade" that is acceptable to stay employed. Also, I think it goes without saying, but any cursing, swearing, shouting or rude remarks made by the rep. on a call or to a staff member will almost always guarantee immediate, on-the-spot termination.

For example, there was a Rep. that had been with a Call Center for eight years. One day, when she received a very challenging call, she desperately tried to keep her composure after giving the same answer, three different ways, so the customer could understand. As the man on the line began screaming at the Rep., she could no longer hold her tongue. She loudly said, "I've already told you three times. It's not my fault if you can't understand the answer. SORRY!!" Unfortunately, the Director of the Center was walking by and heard the conversation. Within ten minutes, the Rep. was called into the Director's office. She then went back to her desk, collected her belongings, and was escorted out of the building by security. Eight years... One call... GONE!!

(<u>So, no losing your shit!!</u>)

Finally, there are the **"occurrences"** used to measure the number of errors that each company allows a Rep. to incur before she is terminated. The "occurrences" usually apply to both the personal metrics and the call metrics of each representative. An occurrence can be a whole number or a fraction. For instance, if you are late coming back from lunch, it could be 1/3 of an occurrence. But if you make a major error on a call or call off from work with no personal time available, it could be 1 whole occurrence.

The list of "whole vs fractional occurrences" can be pages long per company, giving pause on everything a Rep. says and does, once she enters the building each day.

Most companies *used to* allow a Rep. an accrual of 7-9 occurrences before the Rep. was fired. But over the years, that average has shrunk to 5-7 occurrences before the Rep is fired. Some companies will slather off "previous occurrences" after a given amount of time, say 3 months. This lets a Rep. restart from scratch on the total, or at least lessen the total. Other companies *will not* disregard previous occurrences until 6 months or even 12 months later, putting further pressure on the Rep. to be aware of accumulating too many occurrences at once. Otherwise, Boom, fired!!!

So now you can see how the turnover and attrition can go through the roof when it comes to getting and keeping a Rep. in a Call Center. All of this, while she barely earns a minimum wage or slightly above it. Geez, it is exhausting just thinking about it! Whew!!

On the flipside, many of the strict standards and procedures in a Call Center are put in place to manage the call volumes (total number of calls) and the calls in que (on hold). If such standards and procedures are followed correctly by the Reps., they can help to produce an efficient, competent and timely Call Center environment. These are the companies that customers *like* calling into, and they spread the good word to their friends and family regarding their great customer service, which helps the company stay in business, which in turn, produces the revenue needed to pay the Reps. their tiny wages... ahhh, the Circle of Business!!

But these standards can also drive the CALL CENTER GIRLS insane when things go really awry...

Note the following tiny sampling of examples:

- a long call goes into a Rep's break time because the customer can't find her credit card to finish up the sale on a call
- a supervisor casually comes to the Rep's. desk and "mouths" instructions to the Rep. that she doesn't understand, as she also tries to listen to the customer talking directly into her headset
- a rude customer talks non-stop and complains if the Rep. wants to "jump in" and take control of the call
- the computer goes blank, losing all of the information that was just input, and the Rep. must restart and double the time of the call, (without saying a word about the mishap); she cannot seem angry or incompetent to the customer, while she distracts them with some chit chat ("So, how's the weather out there in Chicago today?"), as she quickly re-inputs all the data...uugghh!

These situations can drive a Rep. up a wall!

Just a few examples of the way the Reps. are trying to do the right thing by the customer or management, but taking the "hit for being out of adherence" on any one of the metrics that guide their employment. And since most Reps. average 85-120 calls a day, that's a lot of knots in the stomach that can build up while trying to "make the grade" on every call!!

So the next time you phone into a Call Center for information, or a purchase, or a complaint, <u>please remember, that we Reps., (in a timely fashion, without losing our jobs, or our minds),</u> <u>*are really trying to help you!!*</u>

CHAPTER NINE – "THE FUNNY THINGS"

You can only imagine the number of amusing and/or surprising things we see and hear all day long in a Call Center. Such levity can be a desired relief, especially on the days when the calls seem to be coming in from one pissed complainer to another. Keeping a sense of humor is important in any stressful situation, so it is only befitting for the Reps. to share their crazy, oddball, hilarious calls and anecdotes with one another while on their breaks or in the lunchrooms! Laughing over the absurdity of a call, or smiling over the latest expectations of the staff, while also realizing that you are not alone in this bizarre setting, produces a healthy way of cleansing one's mind of the tension that has built up over the first part of one's shift. It really helps the Rep. to calm down, mentally prepare for the next part of her shift, and make her way back onto the floor in a better mood. Joy, Joy!

Here are some of the most outlandish situations, ridiculous calls and unforeseen circumstances (even amongst the employees) that have actually occurred within a variety of my different Call Centers over the years.

The County Jail Call Center and Switchboard

**** As I left my car in the parking lot each day, I kept my head low, and quickly walked toward the entrance of the Florida County Jail. As I approached the building, I would often encounter two situations before arriving at my desk. First, I would hear the inmates yelling and/or whistling for my attention, as they stared down at me from their jail cell windows on the top floors. Some comments were quite flattering like, "Hey babe, you're looking *fiiiii-ne* today!" Others were downright disgusting, "Hey, you over there with the big tits, come up here and suck my dick!" (Not exactly the warm welcome I wanted to hear at the start of my workday!) Over the months, I became brave and began yelling back at the *mean men* and their comments, saying "At least I'm free to go where I want to, unlike you...ha-ha!" (I certainly would have elaborated on my thoughts in several 4-letter words and hostile phrases, had the surveillance cameras with built-in microphones *not* been around to get ME into trouble!)

The second situation I encountered while entering the Jail was the massive steel doors. Each day, I would have to wait to be buzzed in and out of 3 heavy steel doors, which really slowed me down before finally getting to my desk. I remember looking up at the camera on each closed door, giving the "hurry up" signal to the guard on surveillance so I could make it in on time. Depending on who was on duty, I would either sail through them all, or wait a minute or more on each door by the "jokers" who wanted to make me late. Real Funny Guys!

**** Before suiting up with our headsets at the start of my mid-shift, we would have a briefing in the Jail's training room. There, we would go through a synopsis of the day's events, either regarding the new software that had just been installed on our computers, or a review of any inmates that had been extradited to us from the US Marshall's Office under *alias names*, or we'd have a discussion about the "sweeps" that the Sherriff's Officers were currently putting through on their task forces regarding any DUI's, speeding cars, or drug busts. It was very Hill St. Blues!! And even though we were the support staff in an office environment, in my mind, I always heard, "Let's be careful out there!" at the end of our meeting. 10-4!

**** On my first day in the Inmate Records Division at the Jail, I had no idea how many phone calls I'd be constantly answering on my afternoon/night shift. As soon as the Court closed at 4pm, the fax machine at the Jail would begin to continually print out the reports from each case heard that day. That's also when the phone calls from the public would go into overdrive. Family and friends would want to know the results of each of their beloved's court hearing. Some were pleasantly surprised to learn their loved one was going to be released immediately on their own recognizance, (ROR'd)... "OK, so Jimmy's getting out in an hour. Sweet! Hope he learned his lesson." On the other hand, some were shocked to learn the disappointing fate of their loved one who'd been sentenced to months or years for their crime. "Lordy, Lordy, my brother's in lockup for Christmas? SHIIITT!!"

**** Even though the Reps. were given 30 minutes for lunch at the Jail, and we *could leave* the Jail if we needed to, getting through those steel doors, the security posts in the parking lot, and the traffic lights at the end of the driveway was a veritable hell! By the time you went through that maze and reached the main road, it was time to come back and repeat the process all over again to make it back to your desk on time. Luckily, we were able to either bring in our lunch, or order in food, or go to the Jail's cafeteria.

****As an employee at the Jail, I was given the *opportunity* to have a hot lunch or dinner provided to me free of charge. However, such meals were actually prepared, cooked and served by the "minimum security inmates" that worked in the kitchen. As you can imagine, having seen plenty of movies with prison scenes that had the meals "manipulated" in some fashion, I often wondered whether the food was "clean", free of any disgusting body fluids, foreign objects or powdered drugs that I would regret consuming later in the day. During the few times that I did go to the Jail's kitchen to partake of their wares, I wised up quickly and only ordered what could be made right in front of me the entire time (i.e. fresh scrambled eggs or an omelet, a grilled cheese sandwich, a hamburger made from a frozen patty, etc.). That gave me some sense of control over my choices, as well as the trust that I would not be consuming any additional *"unwanted ingredients"* that may be in the soup, the casserole, the pre-made salads, and alike. YUK!

**** When the Press called to find out about the latest charges on someone *famous* who had just been booked into the Jail, they would try to *bribe* the Rep. with a chance at *fame,* mainly as a Guest on the "News at 11" segment. It's an easy way to get noticed right? Wrong! During our on-the-job training, it was emphasized that, until those new charges became public record, accepting any of those "instant shots to fame" just to leak information would lead to the Rep.'s immediate termination. Not worth it! So, keep on trucking baby!

**** When the inmates are released from Jail, they often use the local taxi service for their rides home. However, it was always interesting to get a call from the public, *not an inmate*, but the public citizens, asking "What's the phone number for the taxi service? I know you know it!" (Seriously, you're calling the Jail to find out what the number is for the taxi cabs?) Really??

<u>The Debit/Credit Card Call Center</u>

**** As a Rep. reporting into a Financial Call Center at 3pm or 4pm in the afternoon, being able to start your *swing-shift on time*, is a feat that cannot be underestimated. This is the shift that starts when the early morning (8am) and mid-morning (11am) people are still there and have not yet finished up but must make room for the next set of Reps. to begin their shift too. As a "Swinger", you must complete the following steps (and keep your sanity), all before taking your first call.

Initially, you must drive in and find an empty parking space, usually on the outskirts of an almost full lot. Secondly, since most Call Centers have a concept called "hoteling", you must find an empty desk. This concept, (where you are *not* assigned a specific desk, just a specific section to sit in depending upon your Call Segment skills) can be daunting when there are missing computers, missing monitors or broken chairs at the empty desks. Many times, you must summon a supervisor to help find a desk with all the working components. Thirdly, if there are no appropriate desks left, you get sent to an "overflow area", usually the training room. There, the Reps. sit at a long table with computers and monitors, within 1 foot of another "elbow mate", and no walls. Headset on, you must do your best to *log in and only listen to your call*, even though you can clearly hear the conversations of all your "neighboring Reps. too." UGH!

**** Working with a customer's available cash balance or credit line becomes a very intimate experience for the both of us. Let's face it: this is usually the one subject that is kept taboo from most of your closest friends and family. And yet, I, a stranger who's only a Rep. on the phone, have the privilege of seeing your assets, debt amounts, credit scores and payment history. (And you didn't even have to buy me dinner?) So, when a call drops (on your end or ours) in the middle of a payment, or a credit limit increase, or a transfer to cover an overdrawn account, we do realize how frustrating the situation is for both of us. This is especially true if there is a high volume of calls and you had been on a very long hold prior to the start of the call. Most of the time we must document the dropped call on your file, only prolonging the call wrap up time for us. So please, be aware of your current reception on your land line phone or your cell phone before placing the call. This way we can both complete your call quickly and correctly. Thanks so much!

**** One day, a customer called in to go over the process of getting a Cash Advance from his credit card. Once the security information and card number were verified, he proceeded to ask in broken English, "How you going to send me to the ATM and pick me up?" (What was he talking about?) He again said, "You gonna get me to ATM and then pick me up?" (Who am I, Scotty from Star Trek, beaming up our customers to and from ATM's for money?) It took another 20 minutes (of my calm, friendly explanations) for this customer to finally understand that it was *his responsibility* to go to an ATM, use his PIN number, and get any Cash Available from his credit card...and we would *not* be picking him up or taking him home!

**** It never ceases to amaze me how many people are up late at night, lonely, and often call into a 24-hour customer service line, just for some comfort and companionship. OK, so where am I going with this? Well, we all know there are plenty of phone numbers out there that provide a certain "type of intimate call girl service" for those wanting a "specific solution" to their "physical needs" late at night (Hell, even the title of this book eludes to that "play on words" for such services!)

However, what I'm talking about is much different. When I worked the overnight shift, I had a customer named "Joanie" who would call in at least twice a week, between 3am and 4am, but only for her current balance on her credit card. She would then proceed to talk non-stop about her business dealings, sales quotas and new clients. I didn't mind hearing her long tales when we were <u>slow</u>, knowing that she was lonely, couldn't sleep, and needed an ear. In exchange, at the end of the call, "Joanie" would always ask for my supervisor and give me a "compliment" to add to my file. These "compliments" were important when it came to tallying up our performance standards and our raises for the year. So, thanks "Joanie" ...and talk on girlfriend!

**** Sometimes Reps. on the night shift can also become "emergency contacts" for our customers. I've received calls from people that have just been beaten up, mugged, assaulted with a weapon, or just felt unsafe in a seedy area! They often want someone to stay on the line with them while they figured out where to go. Although these calls are rare, and can be lengthy, they are also some of the most rewarding for the Reps., when we can calmly notify the local authorities in that area to help them, or do research on the internet where the customer can find immediate help and make them feel safe. Peace of mind...there's nothing like it!

**** Dealing with the "drunks" on an overnight shift at a Call Center can go either way. The "good calls" involve the "happy drunks" that are still partying in the back of a limo and want to swing by and pick you up to join in the fun (even though they're states away)! Or they call in and proceed to tell you at length about their current celebration for their birthday, promotion, anniversary or fill-in-the-blank accomplishment, then thank you over and over again for letting them know they still have credit available on their card to continue to party on…Yay!

However, the "bad calls" involve the "angry drunks" that are trying to pay their bill during last call at a bar, only to have their card blocked for possible fraud or over the limit amounts. Or they've been in a fight with a spouse or a date that has taken their card and who may be on their way to charging large purchases. This is when the Rep. must pull out all of her learned customer service skills to control the call, calmly alleviate the situation, and if possible, unblock the card, increase the limit, or shut down the card to stop any further activity. It can be quite satisfying, when you are the one able to bring down the drunk's *anger* (along with their yelling and screaming) and have them praising you by the end of the call, due to your professionalism and helpfulness! Nice!

**** The most crucial day to use a debit or credit card in the USA is Black Friday. Nothing sparks more people to get up in the middle of the night, venture out into the crowded parking lots, run like cattle to fight over a limited number of "must have widgets *hidden strategically* around the store", stand in eternal lines to finally checkout, just to proceed onto the next venue and repeat the process all over again, all while monitoring an internal clock to get those dramatically reduced "door busters" at each place by the 11am cutoff time!!

Crazy? …yes! Twisted? …sure! However, as a 30 year member of this now infamous cult of discount shoppers, I can honestly say that if one is able to nab that "must have item" at an insanely low, low price during the hunt, while enduring several obstacles on the road to triumph, then it's well worth the effort! And having a "teammate" with you who's willing to play the game as well as you is even more exciting (thanks Sis!), especially when you both finish up your shopping, go relax at the nearest bar, summarize your conquests and discounts over some day drinking, and enjoy an early lunch at 11:15 in the morning, when the battle has finally ceased! Victory!!

BUUUTTT...what happens when you manage to fight that good fight in the store, only to get to the cashier at checkout and have your debit or credit card DECLINED!! WAIT, WHAATT??? (In a panic, you think, I *know* I have plenty of funds available on this card, and it's not expired!!) THEN, WHYYYYY?????

In all of my years in the Call Centers, I have never been screamed at more, or been succinctly called an entire list of curse words on my overnight shift, then when a bevy of customers would call in on Black Friday to say their card was BLOCKED by the bank, at 3, 4, or 5am!! Talk about a possible head explosion...for both of us!

On Black Friday, which is dedicated to the *sacred, early shopper in search of the ultimate bargain*, it can be a colossal blow to have to hold up the checkout line, call the Card Center, and shout into the phone, *"UNBLOCK MY DAMN CARD!!!"* On any other day of the year, the variety of auto-triggers for FRAUD on a card, (time of day, amount of purchase, unusual store location, etc., that those same people would have appreciated), are now creating a frustrating, embarrassing HELL for the customer, who's trying to make that early morning, incredibly priced purchase!! OMG!!!

Next, *the customer must hope* that the Rep. has the *authority* to ask those second layer chosen security questions (and *you* the customer can readily remember the answers to them in your fit of rage), so she's able to *unblock* that "type of fraudulent auto-trigger" that the programmers have put in place, *without* needing further approval from management, causing any further delay in the process to clear the card!

Lots of hurdles to get through to be able to please that very angry, very weary shopper! Heaven forbid if any of those hurdles prevent the Rep. from clearing the card for purchase. At that point the customer must exit the store empty handed...while also leaving their pride at the door...defeated!! Pitiful!

Add to the mix the stores that are now opening *on* Thanksgiving and start selling at 9, 10, 11pm or later. Having that card BLOCKED on Thanksgiving night, after spending a fun, relaxing day with the family, can turn that warm and fuzzy feeling into a raging, pulsating, teeth-grinding shouting match, with who else... the Call Center Rep.!!

So, to all of those discount warriors out there, MY PEOPLE OF THE NIGHT, I beg of you, BEWARE OF THE BLOCKED CARD... and maybe bring some <u>cash</u> along with you too, just in case!!

The Time Share Vacation Sales Call Center

**** Logging in to start your shift at most Call Centers involves typing your user ID and password into the computer, then signing into your "electronic timesheet" for the time stamp. However, at this particular vacation sales call center, using your "fingerprint" was the only way to log in and be accounted for on your time sheet. Unfortunately, when you have fingers that swell in the heat, or have had a various amount of burns from cooking over the years, it is hard to be consistent when placing them on a piece of glass to "read your print". Needless to say, the IT guy and I became fast friends, as we tried to change my "print" to other fingers during my time at this job. We ended up going through 7 of my fingers over 5 months, just so I could log into my shift, my breaks and my exit each day...Yikes!

**** Sales...oy vay! Meeting quotas that can quickly increase each week...along with the knots in your stomach...can be stressful! Such is the life of a Rep. in a Call Center selling mini vacations at time shares! When you are constantly focused on meeting your sales quotas in order to remain employed, you can easily become obsessed with getting that next patron on the line engrossed in your vision of a great vacation at a great location. And watching your co-workers (from your training class) be escorted out of the building each week for *lack of sales* is another reason to do your best on each call! Talk about pressure...Geez!!!

**** Getting that one customer on the phone who's very interested in hearing the perks of a time share vacation package was hard enough! Add to that fact the rule that the supervisors must be the ones to "close" (book) the deal on your phone during your first 6 months, made the "close" even more intense, especially if a supervisor was not readily available nearby. At that point, the Rep. must stand and furiously wave her arms to get the attention of anyone in authority to come over and close before the customer hangs up or the line disconnects, all while remaining calm and pleasant in conversation on the line...Talk about stressful...Yikes!!

The Airport Shuttle Company

**** When booking any rides to the airport at a Shuttle service, it becomes a delicate dance between the Customer and the Call Center Rep. as to when the pickup time at their house or business should commence. To that end, the computer program is the best ally of the Rep., as it works its magic, completing the mathematical calculation of a "recommended pick-up time" based upon the customer's location, their flight time, the drive time allotted to pick up all the passengers booked on the van, as well as the drop-off time at each airline and terminal at the airport. This algorithm has worked efficiently for meeting the customer's needs and satisfaction for over 40 years.

However, there were times when the Reps. would encounter the passenger, (PAX for short), who would plead for an additional 15 or 20 minutes to "sleep in before pick-up". (And so, the dance begins!) The Rep. begins swaying in her tone as she recites the company's disclaimer, stating that the company will not be held responsible if the PAX takes the "time to sleep in", delays the pick-up time, and eventually misses the flight. (2, 3, 4!)

As one of my co-workers once accurately and comically stated to the customer, "So Pumpkin, if you want to delay our "recommended pick-up time for extra sleep" on your fabulous trip to Ireland, the one that you've been dreaming about since you were 12, just to get an additional 15 minutes of sleep, you'd better pray to the gods that it's the right decision, or else you'll be waving to that plane from the airport terminal window as it fades away in the sky. Good Luck!" (Did I mention it was my co-worker's last day in the company? It's why she felt so comfortable being completely honest and sarcastic in her assessment of the situation!) Lucky girl!

**** When a shuttle van that's been picking up passengers suddenly stops working, or has an accident, or is late beyond belief in getting to the last customers, it's the "Rescue Vans" to the RESCUE! (In our minds, they are "ultra- shuttles", with a halo and a cape on the driver, who's dressed in tights, carrying a shield, as he or she saves passengers from missing their flights...GO VAN MAN (OR WOMAN), GO!!!) These "rescue vans" were beckoned most often in the morning, during full-blown gridlock on the roads.

Although the van delays can be legitimate, little did the passenger know that the *driver* was often the cause for the delays, either by oversleeping, or getting breakfast, or getting lost in strange neighborhoods, and/or a combination of excuses. However, it is the Rep. at the Call Center that takes the brunt of the angry, nasty, aggravating calls from the frustrated customers who are about to miss their early AM flights! Those were the days that we Overnight Reps. could not wait until 7:30am..."quittin time"!

**** It's amazing how much people will try to haggle over a small fee! When customers book the airport shuttle van themselves online, they save the $3.00 convenience fee. However, when they called into a Rep. to do the booking for them, they were charged an additional $3.00 convenience fee (which is standard for many industries like the airlines, rental cars, and alike), and usually at a much greater cost. It was then that the battle began for the removal of the fee! Many customers would play the victim, saying they were being penalized for not being able to navigate our online system to complete the booking. Or they didn't have a computer. Or they could not find the website...and so on. The majority of my "adjusted totals" were due to people that did not want to, or simply refused to, pay that minimal $3.00 fee. Therefore, a "one-time courtesy adjustment" was applied, even though many were repeat customers playing the system, and got the discount on every complaint call.

****The attrition (turnover) is quite high in most Call Centers. However, at this particular Call Center, the Director was a sneaky, insecure person, who mistrusted the performances of her Supervisors and Reps. beyond belief! The turnover was always in crisis mode! She would piss off so many of the employees, that even the long term, dedicated ones would quit on the spot after 10 or 15 years with the company, just to finally be relieved of her micro-managing style. For instance, she often walked the aisles herself during the day to correct the phone conversations of her Reps, (usually only done by the Supervisors). Or she took over the call que to rearrange the wait times, (also usually only done by the Supervisors). But the classic move that I was able to personally witness one night was when she actually woke up super early, came into the office through a back door at around 4am and kept the lights off in her office, as she peeked through the mini-blinds out onto the floor just to "catch" any overnight employees that were possibly going against the litany of rules and regulations she had put into place...unbelievable! If she caught the Reps. talking to a co-worker, reading a magazine, or a book, or heaven forbid, checking a cell phone, or searching the internet for anything other than Google Maps, or a bevy of other *child-like don'ts* while waiting for a call to come into the headset. They could be written up or fired on the spot for such behaviors! No wonder we nicknamed her "Mrs. Kravitz", the nosy neighbor from the 60's TV hit "Bewitched" who always "watched everyone" from her house! Crazy!

All of these previous stories represent just a sampling of the funny, silly, crazy and incredibly outlandish incidents that have actually occurred during my many years on the phone lines at the

Call Centers! If you have worked in one, or continue to do so, I'm sure you have your own set of stories and situations that have brought out a wide range of emotions for you too...such is life as a Rep.!

CHAPTER TEN – "MY PERSONAL STORY"

So what the hell happened to me?
How did I end up becoming a "Call Center Girl"?

Well, on my journey, my working years began quite early. It was my senior year of high school, and with all the good grades that I had attained since birth, I was researching local colleges to see where I was going to apply. However, my plans came to an abrupt halt when my father told me that things were going to change quickly in the household. He said that he and my mother were <u>divorcing</u>! That meant I needed to do away with my silly dreams of college, and "go out and get a J.O.B.!!!" Really? I was pissed...and scared. Where was my future going now?

So, I spent my Spring Break canvassing all the corporations in the downtown area of Newark N.J. Early each morning, I walked the 2 miles alone to the bus stop in my hometown, took the 35-minute bus ride into the city, and walked the blocks up and down, filling out applications at all the big and small businesses. Luckily, a week after graduating high school, I immediately started my full-time career at the age of 17 working as a File Clerk in the HQ corporate office of an insurance company. However, the lack of a college education forced me to work longer and harder as a young female, in a male dominated 70's corporate environment, for any and all promotions and rewards that I rightfully deserved. (Think "Mad Men"! Having lived it myself, I still find it hard to watch that show!!)

From there, it was the "Mommy Track", having to leave my job of 12 years that I had grown into from a File Clerk into an Associate Manager over 16 employees. I had literally matured, married and had a baby boy (whom I loved, and still love dearly), during my long-term employment there. Why did I have to leave?

Back then there were no "Formal Daycares" within a 50-mile radius, and most women were never allowed to bring their children to work. This situation was the norm for many of us in the New Jersey/New York area, who were in the working middle class.

So we had to make the big choice...a real Sophie's Choice... of either leaving our jobs after having a child to be a full time Mom, (myself, at 30, which was already 8 years after my friends had their first kids), *or* have a parent or in-law watch their grandchild (ours were all too young and still working themselves), *or* get on a waiting list for a Church child care setting (which were booking a year out or more), *or* just not having a child right away, (making more money to eventually pay a nanny, postponing having a family for a long, long time, hoping your body was still capable of bearing a child and you didn't wait too long). What does one choose? So, I became a full time Mom.

When my son was 18 months old, my husband, son and I moved out of the state of New Jersey (where the interest rates on mortgages were at 13-15%) and headed to Florida. There, we were able to *build* our 1st starter house (at a reasonable price and interest rate). We remained in that first home for 7 years, while I continued on the "Mommy track", taking different low-paying jobs and shifts, working around the schedules of my traveling-salesman husband and my elementary-school-aged child, who was also in many other activities. I was the chauffer, maid, cook, doctor, and handyman of the house too. We were able to save a good amount of money, while getting smart about making some sound investments.

We then moved into a bigger, (older) two story, 4 Bedroom, 2 ½ Bath, Pool Home, also in FL. We really appreciated our new digs and felt so happy to afford such a lavish home that made us all feel like we were staying in a hotel. It was also convenient for travel to the airport, since my husband was now on a plane once or twice a week for daily work trips, or, for 2-3 weeks of training at a time. We remained in that home for 8 years.

Unfortunately, like an old cliché, we slowly grew apart as a couple and as a family. My husband, (the former homebody when I met him), and his inflated ego, now enjoyed the jet set life that he was experiencing on the company's dime away from us. When I asked if he could get a different job within the company with less travel, he scoffed and refused to do so.

Side Note: Ironically, he had no problem obtaining a job with less travel at a different company for the 2nd wife, the c--- he had been having an affair with for 8 months during our marriage, while claiming he always had to leave at 4am for his "Early morning flights"!! Unbelievable! Not cheating on me was the one request I had specifically put forth at the beginning of our marriage (leave me, but don't cheat on me first!). We often laughed about it and swore we would never do anything so terrible to each other in that fashion. HA...what a liar!!

But I digress!!

While my husband and I were still married and he continued to "travel for work" (sometimes legitimately), I began taking classes part time at a Community College, eventually getting my Associate's degree in Hospitality and Tourism Management. Now again, at the time, not knowing what he was doing "on the side", I figured I could get a job in any local FL hotel and provide a supplemental lower income, while I worked my way up to a higher position. I had enjoyed my previous part-time employment in the hotels and knew I could excel in this career. However, had I known how things were about to go down in my marriage, I would have studied a more profitable subject, where I could have made a lot more money.

As I was about to graduate from college, (and just to add to the fun), my husband also ended up committing a heinous, monetary act at his precious job. He came home one night and told me that legal was investigating him at work and that he might be getting fired. I asked if he had done it, and he sternly said an emphatic "NO!" During that week, I kept asking if he input something by accident into the computer, or if someone else could have framed him. I was even to the point of getting a lawyer to prove his innocence and protect his reputation. He would just get angry and say that he knew nothing about what had happened.

On the day that the legal department called him in for a meeting at 10am, he finally admitted to me at 9am that he had committed this act, as he burst into tears. He sobbed, saying that his "ego got the best of him" and that he just wanted to "drive off the bridge and end it all". When I heard that, I volunteered to drive him to work. (Mind you, I was still not aware of his affair at this point). He went into the corporate office for 10 minutes, admitted his guilt, and was fired on the spot, after 9 loyal years. I understood why the company had to do it. And even though I was not happy (I mean, I was really pissed) with his actions at work, I told him that "we would get through it, it was just a job, he was not the job", while I remained loyal to him as my husband. I also said that maybe a fresh start was exactly what we needed to get our lives back on track, away from all the travel.

However, a month later, when he finally admitted that he had been having that long-time affair, that it wasn't a fling, and that he was in LOVE, I was done and told him to leave the house. But before doing so, he had to disclose all of this disgusting information to our son about his being *fired* from his job (not laid off like we had told him as a united front to soften the blow) and about his sleazy affair with his gallivanting whore, since I was not going to be the one to break my 16 year old son's heart.

Talk about a shit storm! The situation was awful. But from the night of his horrible disclosure to me and beyond, I remember being the trooper that I have always been, wiping away my tears, putting on my make-up and my uniform, heading out to my job as a Night Auditor at a hotel, with knives in my stomach, as I greeted the guests and ran my reports. That's what women like me had been trained to do from early on. That's the poker face that I had mastered since my childhood, especially when I had to pretend to ignore my parent's loud arguments during the hot summers, when the windows were all open and everyone in the neighborhood could hear their horrible, violent fights, with the curse words echoing down the block. Horrible!

But again, I digress!

So, with the demise of my own marriage, and the subsequent divorce just as my son was entering his Junior year of High School, I was also fighting for Primary Custody from this sociopathic, selfish man, whom I no longer recognized in character or conviction.

My ex knew that I wanted primary custody, and constantly played a mind-game on me, saying one day, that he would take my son from me for good, and the next day, saying that he wanted him to stay with me since he had "fucked him up enough". It was a roller coaster of emotions each time I had to converse with the man.

During that time, my lawyer advised me to leave my overnight job, "if I truly wanted to qualify for primary custody over an angry 16-year-old boy." So, after only 6 months as a Night Auditor, as well as checking to see if I could move into any other daytime positions at the hotel, and being rejected, I left my job. I was miserable, and slowly going broke. It took another 6 months to sell the house, and besides the little bit of child support and alimony I did get when I attained Primary Custody of my son, I was racking up my credit cards, as I went to each job fair and interview, trying to gain employment during the Great Recession and Housing Bubble of the 2000's! Wretched!

Could he have picked a worse time to have his mid-life meltdown? Absolutely not!! The divorce and final mediation took 9 months, but aged me 10 years. It was brutal! By all accounts it was undeniably the worst time to go through a horrible divorce, sell a depreciating house, then regain a shitty new job and move into an escalated priced apartment, in order to keep my son in the same district of his A-Rated High School!! I'm surprised an epidemic didn't hit too…oh wait, it did…West Nile Virus from the mosquitos in FL! Luckily that was the one thing we were spared during this treacherous time in our lives!

It took me a year to find full time employment again…and this time it was at…wait for it… the County Jail! Low and Behold, this is where I was introduced to the fine art of the Call Center!!

That's right, I was now part of the local government as an Inmate Records Clerk. So, I began yet another new adventure in my career, learning about the codes, terms and sentencing used in the criminal justice system. Once I was trained, I began wearing my first headset for at 6 least hours during an 8-hour shift. I won't lie, it was quite uncomfortable at first, with the headphones making my ears sore, as I clumsily learned the volume control button, (which becomes your best friend for loudness or softness per call). It took about a week before I eventually got the hang of it all.

I fielded calls from the general public, wanting to know what the charges were on a new arrest, or when the inmate was being released or bonded out. I ended up staying there only for a year, since my promotion would have had me becoming an Intake Deputy. That involved booking in the latest arrests, while wearing a hideous uniform, carrying a gun, and having my hair tied up in a bun all night. No thank you!!

So, I picked up and went onto the next Call Center. I was offered a job on the spot with a substantial increase in pay dealing with the debit and credit cards from 600 different credit unions across the US. I was able to stay 5 years in that job on an overnight shift, until the rumors spread that the division was moving to AZ. That was my cue to start interviewing and move onto my next job before the pink slips! (The division did eventually move to AZ, leaving many of my former co-workers out of work for quite a bit of time).

However, within 3 weeks of those initial rumors of moving to AZ at the Call Center, I jumped again and took a job at a Car Loan Company in FL. I was now doing Auto Loans, working as a Loan Processor. I was verifying the legal docs, attaining the needed funds from our financial partners, closing out the final signed documents, while also following all the rules and regulations from the State. However, I also had to wear my trusty headset when answering the calls from our customers, our banks, our credit unions, and the other employees. I remained at this job for 1 ½ years, until they were selling the building and closing the branch. So once again I had to jump before the layoffs!! (No funny stories to share either...it was all business!)

At this point, I was tired of going through all the shuffling from job to job in FL. So, I decided to finally plan for and make the big jump to the one place that I had been dreaming of moving to for over 20 years, married or not...

Las Vegas, baby!!

By this time, my son was done with all his college years, including his Master's Degree. It was great to see him settle into his new High School as an AP Human Geography Teacher. It was two hours away in another part of FL. With that in mind, I felt it was finally time for me to pack up and make the bold move to Las Vegas, NV, a place that I had been visiting and enjoying for 30 years. However, I knew no one out there, and most of my friends and family thought I was crazy for even thinking about going it alone. But I remained focused, did my research, and construed a 6-month plan to put a deposit on a great Vegas apartment. I saved for my airline ticket, the shipping of my boxes and my car, and had an estate sale in FL to sell off everything else I no longer wanted from my crumbled marriage. It was time to make a minty fresh start!

On my final weekend in FL., I had a going away party at my favorite karaoke bar to celebrate my previous 25 years of living there. I was shocked to see how many people came out to wish me well on my new adventure. It was such a fun night and remains a cherished memory.

My journey had multiple stops that I had planned along the way. First, I landed and detoured through many towns in New Jersey for 11 days, staying with my aunt, but renting a car and visiting all my "original" hometown friends and co-workers. Really Good Times! Then I re-boarded and flew into Atlanta, Georgia. This time I spent a week in the area, visiting cousins and friends that had moved there in prior years. It was a long time coming, finally getting to see all of them and their fabulous houses. Again, Good Times! I then flew the last leg to my final destination...Las Vegas. I settled in nicely to my fabulous one-story, one bedroom apartment with an attached garage. I unpacked, set up my few belongings, and was sending out resumes within a week's time. I was home!!

When I arrived in Las Vegas, the economy was still flailing from the Great Recession, just like in FL. The unemployment rate was still quite high. I knew I was going to try for the higher paying Administrative jobs at first where I had a great deal of experience. After 5 weeks, I applied to all the local hotels in Las Vegas. But, with only four interviews and no job offers, I was getting nervous. My money was now tight, so I had to apply for anything, just to get hired. Enter another Call Center!!

I answered the ad for a "Vacation Outbound Sales Advisor" at a Resort Ownership Company. This was a fancy title for a job in a Call Center environment. I was once again hired on the spot and started the following week. This time I was selling mini vacations at discount prices. This was a great way for entire families to stay in the 4- or 5-star resorts and enjoy all of the amenities, as long as they agreed to go on a 2-hour timeshare sales tour during their stay. The tours are where the salesmen really try to convince people that this is the best way to vacation with the family, year in and year out, while having a choice of the 10 different US resorts that were part of their fabulous group of properties.

Side Note Disclosure: I have never been comfortable working in "Sales" for any product, in any company, or any bake sale, or any garage sale, or even just to upsell or upgrade a reservation or telephone package... YUK!! Meeting a company's sales quota that may start at 3 weekly sales when you are new, and quickly escalate to 12 weekly sales or more after 6 weeks on the job before you hear, "you're fired", can be such a life stressor! To get that many sales, a phone Rep. normally must be persuading the customer to buy on 600-800 calls per week, just to claim 3 or 4 sales. Mind Blowing!!

However, since I needed the job and the money really bad at this point, I knew that I could fully support the nature of selling these mini vacations to the timeshares. Why? Because back in the day, I was a woman that had bought, taken, and thoroughly enjoyed several of those mini vacations with my family for years, especially during our first 10 years of living in Fl. I would figure out the best deals to get the most luxurious suites, meal vouchers and tickets to shows, all included in the low, low price of $109 for a 4-day, 3-night stay, for 3 people near Disneyworld. In fact, my husband and I bought a time share during our marriage and used it in conjunction with his points for free airfares. We traveled with our son throughout the US, the Bahamas, and even Europe, over a 10-year period. It was fabulous!

Once hired, and despite all my hotel and resort experience, I was barely eking out my sales quotas each week, and I constantly had the feeling of knives in my stomach to prove it. But I was doing so much better than most of my co-workers from my class, who one by one, were being escorted out, week after week for their lack of sales.

One Sunday, my sister called me from FL. She was upset, so I asked right away "What's the matter?" She told me she had just gone through a battery of health tests for an elective surgery she was thinking of having done. The results were in and they were devastating...two types of cancer were found in separate parts of her body. She was only 53 years old. On top of which, she had just finalized her divorce 3 months earlier, and had sole custody of her own 14-year-old daughter.

Besides having my grown son locally in FL, but still over 2 hours away from my sister, there were no other family members there to help her out. I spent the next 3 days trying to figure out how I could stay in Vegas, while also helping my sister with her doctor's appointments, surgeries, recoveries and follow-up treatments.

After 3 sleepless nights, I knew what I had to do. So, I went into the Call Center early the next morning with my headset back in its box. As I was signing my resignation with HR, I was given the Employee of the Month Certificate and a $25 gift card to Chili's. Despite all those feelings of knives in the stomach, I was proud to see that I had proven myself in the sales position. I broke into laughter, then anxious tears, as I apologized for my quick departure. The HR girls were great, while they comforted me through my emotional pain.

Within a week, I had donated my new bed and TV to Goodwill, gave away my dinette set for $50, and shipped the 10 boxes that contained "my life" back to FL. I put the car back on a cross country carrier and boarded the plane bound for FL. Two days after arriving back in FL, my mother, who was in a nursing home in NJ, caught a bad infection. Despite their best efforts at two different hospitals, she was not able to recover and passed away 3 weeks later. Sadly, it was 4 days before my sister's first cancer surgery. She had already waited a month preparing for it. So, through several conference calls to the nursing home and funeral parlor in NJ, we were able to plan a lavish funeral mass for our mother, but we were not able to attend, since it was on the day before the surgery. It was just awful for my sister, myself and our children to be faced with such another "Sophie's Choice" decision. However, we knew that our mother would have wanted us to move forward with the health care. It would be another 2 years before we would get the all clear on my sister's health and I would make my final journey back to Las Vegas!

In the meantime, I took my final Call Center job in FL. This time it was as an overnight Rep. for an airport shuttle company. I was not making much, but it was a way to help pay down my moving bills and start saving for my future, while I continued to care for my sister and her appointments during the day. I was now back on the graveyard shift doing the booking, modifying and canceling of reservations for the Van rides to and from the airports. Out of all the Call Center jobs that I had worked in previously, this one was certainly the easiest, and the most fun on an overnight shift. Per usual, I was grateful that I was hired quickly, passed the assessment test, and started earning money within a week's time. I remained there for 10 months before moving back to Las Vegas! Once I settled in, I took a fabulous Administrative job with the State of Nevada... a complete change from the previous Call Centers! YAY!!

CHAPTER ELEVEN – "FINAL THOUGHTS"

The **"secrets"** and **"confessions"** that I have noted throughout this book are quite eye opening, but perhaps all too familiar to other women out there who have been reading them. The life stories told here evoke the tales of how many of us become "stagnant" when forced to *leave* the workplace for a while, mainly for our families. Or how we can become "stuck in a rut" while *staying in* the workplace. As women, many of us are challenged by the multiple transitions during our lives (whether expected or unexpected) which prevent us from moving up as quickly as others, or as high up as others, in the workforce. And after any number of years, we can still find it difficult to keep up with our "Mommy" duties at home, while also accurately performing the duties at our full time or part time jobs.

As we age, the working game changes again.

According to different articles published in the "Senior" magazines, factors that may affect the *slowdown* of a woman's further potential at work are:

- not having a higher education in place (Bachelor or Master's)
- not being in the company as long as the men doing the same work
- not being able to stay late for special projects when family calls
- not having learned the new software programs or social media outlets that are familiar to others, but did not exist years ago when she began

- not being as young as everyone else in the office
- not being as healthy and energetic to keep up with the long hours

Moving on to a new job after having a baby, or moving out of state before the layoffs and closures begin, or moving back home when a family member becomes ill and needs your help, can make you feel like a "galloping gypsy" (or a criminal on the run!!). But no matter *where* we women live or work, it's amazing to see what jobs we will take to continually make a legitimate buck and avoid the unemployment line!!

For me, doing the "Call Center Dance" became my way of taking the open opportunities to again get my foot in the door at each unforeseen turn in my life. However, as each Call Center moved away or closed down in the area in which I lived in Fl., I had to keep moving on myself.

To sum it all up, during the past 10 years, I have spent a great deal of time working in 5 different "Call Center Girl" environments. And despite the gruesome facts and figures that I have divulged to you about the daily life of a woman in a Call Center, I have nothing but the greatest respect for the Reps., Supervisors and Managers who continue to *thrive* in those stressful 24/7 Call Center environments. Yay You!!!

I would also like to take this opportunity to express my deepest gratitude to those companies who decided to take a chance on me by bringing me into their work families over the years and allowing me to thrive on the job!

I will always be grateful for the immediate hiring, the late night or overnight shifts (my favorite!!), the beautiful friendships that I established with my co-workers, the hospitable knowledge I acquired in creating a great phone call experience, and the feeling of purpose that I obtained while working in each Call Center, especially when I was going through my own personal struggles. Finally...

I will always fondly remember what it was like to be a
Call Center Girl!!

Thank you for calling (fill in the company).
My name is Donna!
How may I help you today?